WELCOME TO FLORIDA

CARTOONS BY HORTOON

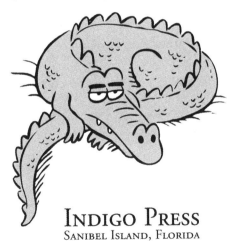

D1552843

INDIGO PRESS
SANIBEL ISLAND, FLORIDA

Welcome to Florida, Cartoons by Hortoon © 2011 by David Horton.

Published by: Indigo Press L.C.
     2560 Sanibel Boulevard
     Sanibel, Florida 33957

ISBN - 9780982967409
Library of Congress Control Number: 2011941427

Visit Hortoon.com for new Cartoons, T-shirts and other Fun Stuff.

A special thanks to Adam Bauer, the talented artist who colorized the cartoons and made this book even better with his creative ideas and twisted sense of humor.

First-edition paperback printing, November 2011.

INDIGO PRESS
SANIBEL ISLAND, FLORIDA

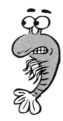

For Diane

2

3

5

7

HORTOON

HORTOON

10

11

14

15

16

17

19

21

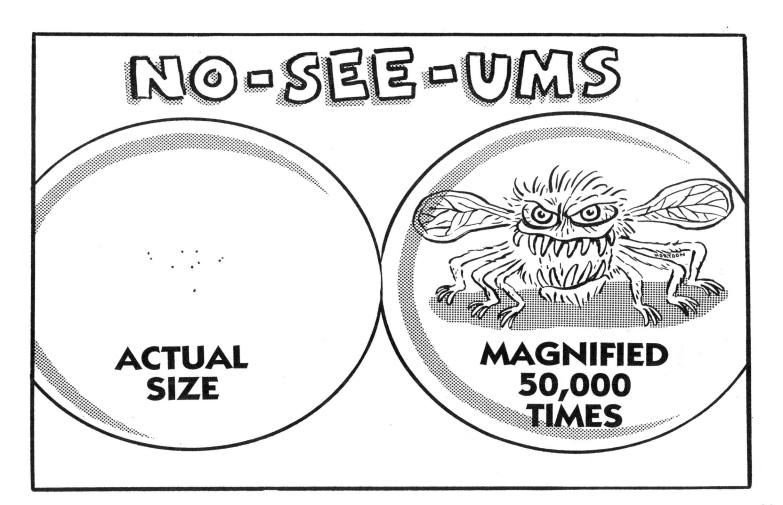

24

25

26

28

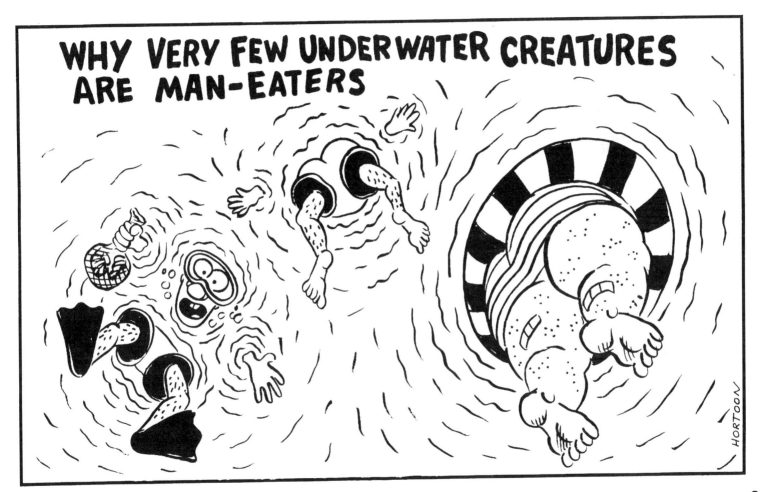

31

HORTOON

35

36

38

39

41

42

43

45

47

48

49

50

51

53

54

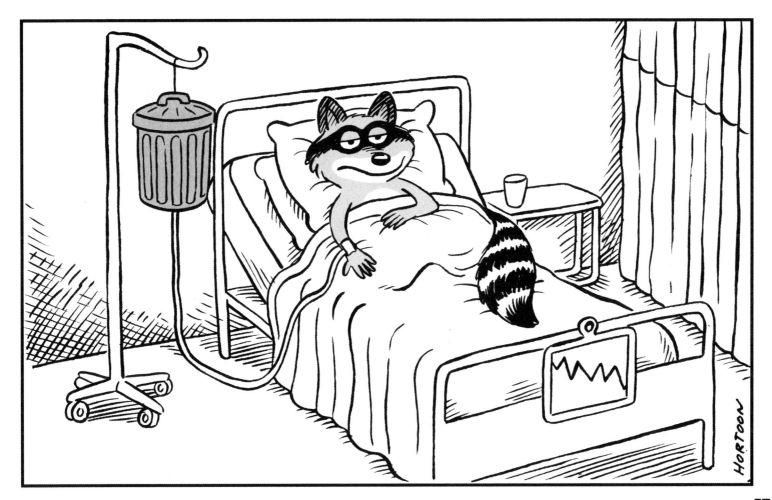

61

63

64

66

69

73

74

75

80

TO AVOID AIRLINE BAG CHARGES, THE HORNSTEIN FAMILY DECIDES TO WEAR ALL THEIR VACATION CLOTHES.

82

HORTOON

86

87

89

AFTER YEARS OF TOURISTS ABUSING THE LIVE SHELL RULE ON THE BEACH, LIVE SHELLS DECIDE TO GET EVEN...

93

94

95

98

101

Clean up my yard?!
I would never destroy the natural habitat of these wonderful creatures!

106

111

115

CANS NEWSPAPER GLASS PLASTIC LEFTOVERS

HORTOON

The Dracula Family Vacation

127

131

CLICK!

HORTOON

133

134

TREE DECORATING THE FLORIDA WAY

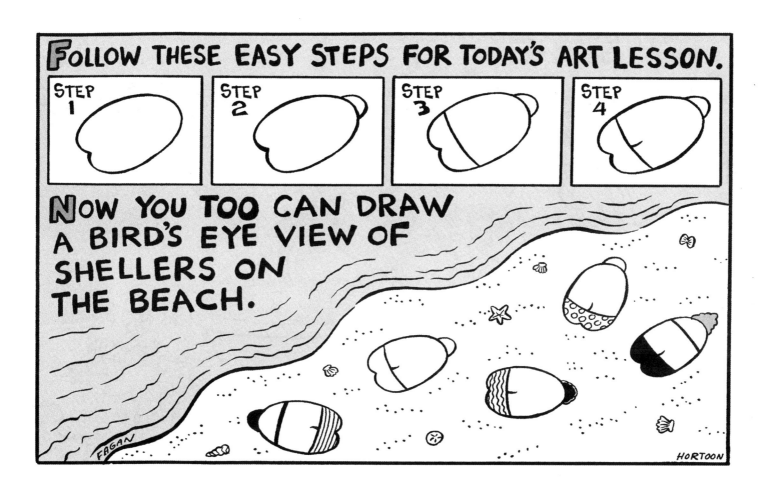

138

MOST FLORIDA RESIDENTS GET A SINISTER SMILE ON THEIR FACE THIS TIME OF YEAR

159

HORTOON

160

RACCOON
HEAVEN

HORTOON

162

167

169

174

176

THE REALITY OF A FAMILY GETTING READY FOR DINNER IN A SINGLE BATHROOM VACATION RESORT

HORTOON

177

A SNEAKY FLORIDA SIGHTSEER...

SEA SHELL SALE!

BIG BAG O' SHELLS

BAG O' SHELLS

BIG BAG O' SHELLS

178

180

183

Some called them naive, others stupid... but brothers **Tom** and **Nick** never realized the annual **PETA** party was a poor time to show off their **new hats.**

www.garbage.com

HORTOON

186

189

HORTOON

196

199

205

Following are a few sketches that provide a window into the weird world of Hortoons.

Most of these doodles never became full-fledged cartoons, proving either too unfinished or too twisted for newspaper editors to publish.

They're published now!

209

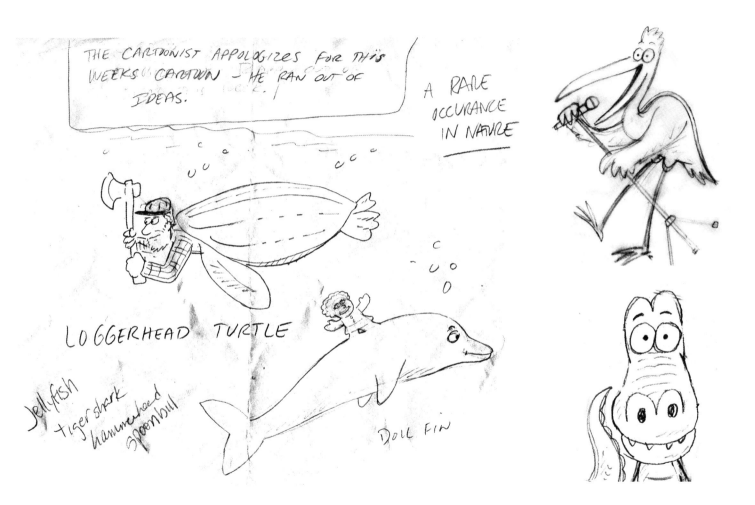

THE CARTOONIST APPOLOGIZES FOR THIS WEEKS CARTOON — HE RAN OUT OF IDEAS.

A RARE OCCURANCE IN NATURE

LOGGERHEAD TURTLE

Jellyfish
Tigershark
Hammerhead
Spoonbill

DOLL FIN

215

216

- THE ALLIGATOR WHISPERER

The End